1. Introduction

The idea that high prices and large amounts of (mainly) dissipative advertising[2] may serve to separate high-quality firms from the their *actual* low-quality competitors seems widespread. However, the theoretical demonstration of this has remained rather elusive, in the sense that formal modelling has (to the best of our knowledge) focused exclusively on the monopoly case.[3] For the monopoly case, the influential, seminal study by Milgrom and Roberts (1986) has shown that a high introductory price and a strictly positive level of dissipative advertising may serve to reveal the high quality of a new experience good. Thus, this particular combination of price and advertising allows a high-quality monopolist to escape the shadow of its hypothetical low-quality cousin.[4] However, the low-quality firm remains hypothetical, and consumers only observe one pair of price and advertising signals from which to draw information.

In this paper we study a model with two actual competitors, where one has high quality and the other low quality. The incompletely informed consumers thus observe two pairs of price and advertising signals from which to draw information. The aim of the study is to investigate whether the qualitative features alluded to at the beginning may arise in equilibrium in a duopoly setting. Our general starting point is that this is far from obvious. On the one hand, separation via a high price may be a costly strategy for a high-quality firm, since a large fraction of customers may be

---

[2] The term "dissipative advertising" refers to advertising expenditures that potentially signal quality to consumers within the context of a signaling game. That is, the firms essentially burn money to make a point. This is in contrast to other potential roles that advertising might serve such as directly conveying information to consumers or attempting to influence their preferences.

[3] A partial exception is Matthews and Fertig (1990). Using equilibrium notions related to ours, they consider sequential advertising signals by a potential entrant and an incumbent firm. However, prices do not simultaneously serve as signals.

[4] For various alternative analyses of quality signaling in the monopoly case, see e.g. Ramey (1987), Lutz (1989), Bagwell and Riordan (1991), Bagwell (1992), Hertzendorf (1993, 1996), Overgaard (1993, 1994), and Horstman and MacDonald (1994).

lost to its low-quality competitor.[5] On the other hand, if prices are strategic complements, a successful separating strategy might dampen the intensity of price competition, resulting in higher profits to both the high-quality and the low-quality firm as compared to a case of intensive Bertrand-style competition between suppliers of products that are perceived homogenous by consumers at the time of purchase. On a priori grounds, it is far from clear how these incentives trade off in equilibrium, and which role might be played by advertising. The paper thus represents a first attempt to extend the existing literature by allowing actual price and advertising competition between vertically differentiated oligopolists.

This paper is a natural extension of earlier work reported in Hertzendorf and Overgaard (1998) where just price signaling is studied in a duopoly setting. The study of signaling phenomena in competitive environments is complicated by the absence of an obvious and tractable game form. We therefore propose a simple model with two firms, and where Nature randomly (in the sense of flipping a fair coin) assigns one firm to be the high-quality firm and the other to be the low-quality firm. The potential customers are assumed to know this, but they do not know which firm offers the high quality. In contrast, a firm knows its own quality, as well as that of its rival.[6] For the present purposes we believe that the assumption that there is exactly one firm offering a high quality and one firm offering a low quality is a natural one to make. In particular, if we believe that the quality of each firm is determined by some stochastic process exogenous to the model, then it certainly makes sense to assume that the probability that the two qualities coincide exactly is zero. If firms have different qualities, then it follows logically that one firm offers a high quality and one firm offers low quality. Furthermore, we believe that in many situations, determining the quality of a rival will be an exercise associated with negligible costs for a firm. Essentially, we assume that each firm has sufficient expertise and/or testing facilities to undertake analysis or testing that is not available to the typical consumer. Hence, our assumption that each firm knows the quality of its rival, but potential customers

---

[5] In a monopoly signaling game sales might also be lost as the result of price signaling, but not to a competitor.

[6] These assumptions are similar to assumptions made by Gabszewicz and Grilo (1992), who study a similar problem in a non-signaling context.

do not know which firm offers which quality.[7]

The signaling model analyzed below is adopted from a standard complete information model.[8] Initially, the potential customers have a diffuse prior as to which firm offers the high quality. On observing two pairs of price and advertising signals, the customers update their beliefs and make their purchasing decisions accordingly. Consumers are assumed to be heterogenous, but they all prefer a high quality. There is a continuum of consumers whose reservation values for a given quality are distributed on some interval. The "address" of a consumer together with the given quality indicates how much utility a consumer would obtain from consuming one unit priced at zero (i.e., the potential gains from trade). We shall assume that consumers purchase a maximum of one unit of the good from either the low or the high quality firm, depending on which purchase, if any, maximizes their utility (or expected utility). Full details of the model, including our definition of equilibrium, are discussed in the next section. However, the most significant results of our research can be summarized:

1. Unlike in the typical monopoly signaling game, the complete information price profile can never *by itself* separate the two qualities; that is, separation is always associated with distortions of either price, advertising or both.

2. In contrast to the monopoly case, the prices of *both* qualities are distorted in separating equilibria. This follows from the strategic complementarity of prices when competition is *actual* rather than hypothetical. The direction of the distortion in prices depends on the magnitude of the difference in quality between the two firms.

3. If the degree of vertical differentiation is large, signaling will be done by price alone, while if the difference in quality is

---

[7] It is, of course, harder to justify the assumption that consumers know the actual values of high and low quality, but not their assignment to firms. However, this assumption is routinely made in the literature on monopoly games, and is not peculiar to this study. Addressing this objection head-on forms an interesting topic for future research.

[8] Models similar to the one considered here were developed by Gabszewicz & Thisse (1979, 1980) and Shaked & Sutton (1982, 1983).

below a key threshold, advertising signals are used to convey information about quality. If only price is used to signal quality, *both* prices are necessarily distorted upwards, while if advertising is used, prices may be distorted below complete information levels.

4. With price and advertising available as signals, separating equilibria always exist even though the profit functions of the two firms are, a priori, identical; that is, the game is non-generic in a generalized sense of the abstract literature on two-player signaling games. If only prices are available as signals, separating equilibria only exist if the degree of vertical differentiation is sufficiently large.

A comparison of this paper with the previous work reported in Hertzendorf and Overgaard (1998) sheds important light on the role of advertising. Unlike the case where only price signals are permitted, the introduction of advertising admits a separation of the two qualities even when the quality difference is arbitrarily small. As an empirical matter, the analysis below suggests that dissipative advertising may have its most important role as a signal of quality exactly in this case rather than in the case where the two qualities are dramatically different. This conclusion appears to comport well with the empirical evidence for many experience goods whether they be breakfast cereals, soft drinks or internet access.

The introduction of advertising also implies that separating equilibrium prices are not always higher than under complete information. On the contrary, the signaling of product quality may result in the high quality firm reducing its price while advertising "heavily." When the price of the high-quality firm is reduced, so is the price of the low-quality firm due to the strategic complementarity of prices in the underlying Bertrand competition. This would seem to contradict the naive perception that advertising expenditures result in inflated prices since those expenditures must be recovered from sales to consumers. This result has important empirical implications. For example, to the extent that advertising plays a role in signaling the quality of tobacco products, our results suggests that (holding taxes fixed, and in the absence of collusion) a ban on tobacco advertising has the capacity to increase prices.

Our results also show that the relationship between the degree of vertical differentiation and the (separating) advertising

5

expenditures of the high-quality firm is subtle, whereas the low-quality firm never advertises in separating equilibrium. When the quality difference between the two firms is large, there is no advertising. Instead, there is pure price signaling. When the difference becomes somewhat smaller, the advertising expenditures of the high-quality firm are positive and increasing while its price decreases. As the quality difference decreases even further, at some point the advertising expenditures peak and start decreasing toward zero as the products become closer substitutes in consumption. Hence, the (separating) equilibrium advertising expenditures of the high-quality firm are non-monotonic in the degree of vertical differentiation.

The relationship between the level of advertising and the degree of vertical differentiation can be explained as follows. When the difference in quality between the two firms is great, price increases are a more efficient signaling mechanism (i.e., less costly) than advertising. This is because a price increase by the high-quality firm has two effects. First, it increases the profits to the low-quality firm from not mimicking. In fact, the low-quality firm will face increased demand as the result of a price increase and, therefore, increase its own price in response. Second, it reduces the profits from mimicking since there is reduced demand at the higher price now charged by the high-quality firm. In comparison, an advertising signal has only one effect; it increases the cost of mimicry.

When the difference in quality is less, price signaling is too costly to be employed by the high-quality firm. When the two goods are close substitutes, the demand for the high-quality good is highly elastic. The loss in demand associated with a small price increase renders price signaling unattractive. Hence, the high-quality firm substitutes advertising signals for price signals. As the degree of vertical differentiation approaches zero, the benefits from separation also approach zero since consumers view the two goods as close substitutes. The high-quality firm responds by spending less and less on advertising. The non-monotonic relationship between the level of advertising and the degree of vertical differentiation suggests that empirical tests of the signaling hypothesis must be carefully designed.

Finally, the paper is novel in the sense that by using two simple and natural equilibrium refinements we uncover a unique separating equilibrium profile and a unique pooling equilibrium profile. The first refinement, which may be viewed as a restricted version of Bagwell and Ramey's (1991) unprejudiced beliefs, allows a selection on the set of separating profiles while preserving existence. The second prunes the set of pooling profiles to a single point reminiscent of a zero-profit Bertrand outcome. These refinements should be useful to other researchers with a general interest in multi-sender signaling games.

The paper is organized as follows. Section 2 sets out our simple underlying model of a vertically differentiated duopoly and explains the structure of information in the two-sender signaling game. Section 3 defines our basic notion of equilibrium and characterize the set of equilibria. In Section 4 we briefly discuss the added difficulties of equilibrium selection in multi-sender contexts, introduce two simple refinements and characterize the profiles that survive refinement. The results are further discussed in Section 5, while Section 6 contains some concluding remarks. The Appendix contains a collection of proofs.

2. The Model

In this section we outline the basic assumptions of a simple duopoly signaling game. There are two competing firms, and the nature of the game can be described as follows: Nature makes the first move by randomly assigning one of the firms to be the high-quality firm and the other to be the low-quality firm. Each firm has an equal probability of being selected by Nature to produce the high-quality product. This assignment is known to each firm but not (at least initially) to consumers. However, the probability distribution of Nature's choices is common knowledge. Each firm then simultaneously adopts a price and advertising strategy. Both strategies are simultaneously observed by consumers who then make their purchasing decisions. Although consumers are initially unaware of Nature's assignment, the strategies adopted by the two firms, if different, will signal to consumers which firm is which. The two possible levels of quality (H and L) are scalars known beforehand by consumers. For a given price consumers always prefer the high-quality product. However, if the low-quality product is sold at a lower price, some consumers prefer to purchase the low-quality product.

We assume that there is a continuum of potential consumers with a uniform distribution of valuations. Each consumer buys at most one unit and has a well-defined utility function $U_\theta = \theta Q - p$, where $\theta \in [0,1]$ represents the "address" of the consumer, $Q \in \{L, H\}$ where $L < H = 1$, and p is the price paid by the consumer. We assume that $\theta \sim unif[0,1]$, and that the total mass of consumers is one. When consumers know the quality of the firm they are purchasing from, it is easy to determine the demand faced by each firm for a given set of prices. That is, consumers will potentially purchase from a given firm if, at the firm's price, positive utility results. If purchasing from the firm of quality Q results in greater utility for a given consumer than a purchase from the firm of quality K, then the consumer only purchases one unit from firm Q. Consumers associated with high thetas value quality more and, hence, are more likely to purchase from the high quality firm than the low-quality firm. In fact, for a given set of prices (p_L, p_H), there is a unique θ^* which separates consumers who wish to purchase from the high-quality firm from those who wish to purchase from the low-quality firm (i.e., $\theta^* - p_H = L\theta^* - p_L$). There is also a unique θ^{**} which separates the consumers who purchase from the low-quality firm from those consumers who make no purchases (i.e., $L\theta^{**} - p_L = 0$).

Provided that $0 < \theta^{**} < \theta^{*} < 1$, we can write the demands facing the high-quality and low-quality firms as functions of the price set by each respective firm and the price of its rival. To simplify the analysis, the quality of the high-quality firm is assumed to be 1, and the exogenous parameter $L < 1$ (the quality offered by the low-quality firm), by default, captures the quality difference between the two firms. In the notation below, the subscript represents the actual type of firm, while the superscript captures consumer expectations of quality. Under complete information the demands are as follows[9]:

$$D_H^H(p_H, p_L, L) = 1 - \theta^{*} = 1 - \frac{p_H - p_L}{1 - L} \qquad D_L^L(p_L, p_H, L) = \theta^{*} - \theta^{**} = \frac{p_H - p_L}{1 - L} - \frac{p_L}{L}.$$

The condition $0 < \theta^{**} < \theta^{*} < 1$ ensures that both firms sell goods to consumers in equilibrium. It is straightforward to show that, in any of the equilibria we will consider below, this in fact will be the case.

The demand functions above assume that consumers know which firm offers which quality. As noted, this would be the case under complete information. It would also be the case in a separating equilibrium where the two firms adopt different strategies. However, if the low-quality firm mimics the strategy of the high-quality firm, consumers will be unable to distinguish one firm from the other. In this situation consumers (with sufficiently high θ's) randomly purchase from either firm under the assumption that it offers a level of quality equal to $(H+L)/2 = (1+L)/2 \equiv \rho$. If the low-quality firm mimics the strategy of the high-quality firm (in order to leave consumers uninformed) the demand faced by both firms is:

$$D_Q^\rho(p, p, L) = (1/2)\left(1 - \frac{2p}{1+L}\right) \qquad Q \in [L, H]$$

In this case, the equal sharing of demand when prices are uninformative gives the model a standard Bertrand-flavor. This will be exploited below when we study pooling equilibria. Likewise, the high-quality firm must determine whether or not to adopt a strategy that is too costly for the low-quality firm to mimic. As we will show below this will entail the high-quality firm changing its price from the complete information price and/or spending money on advertising. We can now proceed with the

---

[9] Further details can be found in Hertzendorf and Overgaard (1998). Similar modelling was initially developed by Gabszewicz and Thisse (1979, 1980) and Shaked and Sutton (1982, 1983).

9

analysis.

First, an additional assumption and some additional notation must be introduced. We shall assume throughout that unit costs are constant across qualities and normalized to zero. Then we can define the duopoly profits of each firm in the obvious manner by taking the demand functions given above and multiplying by the respective price charged by the given firm. Of course the demand actually faced by each firm depends on whether or not they ultimately adopt identical strategies. We express this fact by making the profit function of each firm a function of consumer beliefs. In particular, profits are contingent on *posterior* consumer beliefs represented by $\mu((p_Q, A_Q), (p_K, A_K))$, where $\mu: [0,1]^2 \times \Re_+^2 \rightarrow [0,1]$.[10] We interpret $\mu((p_Q, A_Q), (p_K, A_K))$ as the posterior consumer probability assessment that the firm adopting the strategy (p_Q, A_Q) offers a high-quality product for sale, given that the other firm has adopted the strategy (p_K, A_K). Since consumers know that there is one firm of each type, the assessments across the firms must sum to one, and it follows that $\mu((p_Q, A_Q), (p_K, A_K)) = 1 - \mu((p_K, A_K), (p_Q, A_Q))$. We use the following notation to present the profits of a given firm of quality Q:

$$\Pi_Q(p_Q, p_K, A_Q, \mu((p_Q, A_Q), (p_K, A_K)), L) = p_Q D_Q^\mu(p_Q, p_K, L) - A_Q$$

In this notation, the last element, L, in Π_Q is an exogenous parameter which represents the quality level of the low-quality firm (recall that H is normalized to 1). The second to last element represents the probability assessment that the firm which has adopted the first strategy (i.e. (p_Q, A_Q)) is the high-quality firm. We assume that advertising has no direct effect on demand. Advertising can only affect the demand faced by a given firm by changing consumer beliefs. In other words, holding beliefs fixed, neither firm would ever advertise since it reduces profits. In signaling game terminology: advertising is a dissipative signal. On the other hand, prices have a direct effect on demand even if consumer beliefs are fixed.

_____

[10] Without loss of generality, we assume that prices are in the unit interval. Given the specification of utilities, no consumer would visit an outlet charging a price in excess of one.

3. Analysis

Throughout the paper we shall restrict attention to pure strategy equilibria, and our basic notion of equilibrium is defined below.

Definition 1: An equilibrium is a pair of price-advertising strategies $(\hat{p}_L, \hat{A}_L)$ and $(\hat{p}_H, \hat{A}_H)$ and a system of beliefs $\mu((p_Q, A_Q), (p_K, A_K))$ such that:

(1) $(\hat{p}_L, \hat{A}_L) \in \arg \max \Pi_L(p_L, \hat{p}_H, A_L, \mu((p_L, A_L), (\hat{p}_H, \hat{A}_H)), L)$ with

$p_L \in [0, 1]$ and $A_L \geq 0$

(2) $(\hat{p}_H, \hat{A}_H) \in \arg \max \Pi_H(p_H, \hat{p}_L, A_H, \mu((p_H, A_H), (\hat{p}_L, \hat{A}_L)), L)$ with

$p_H \in [0, 1]$ and $A_H \geq 0$

(3) if $(\hat{p}_L, \hat{A}_L) \neq (\hat{p}_H, \hat{A}_H)$ then $\mu((\hat{p}_H, \hat{A}_H), (\hat{p}_L, \hat{A}_L)) = 1$

(4) if $(\hat{p}_H, \hat{A}_H) = (\hat{p}_L, \hat{A}_L)$ then $\mu((\hat{p}_H, \hat{A}_H), (\hat{p}_L, \hat{A}_L)) = 1/2$

(5) $\mu((p_H, A_H), (p_L, A_L)) + \mu((p_L, A_L), (p_H, A_H)) = 1$

Condition (1) merely requires that the low-quality firm selects a strategy that maximizes its profits, taking as given the strategy of the high-quality firm and the beliefs of consumers (i.e., *sequential rationality*). Similarly, condition (2) requires that the high-quality firm selects a strategy that maximizes its profits, taking as given the strategy of the low-quality firm and the beliefs of consumers. Requirements (3) and (4) capture that beliefs have to make sense given the strategies of the firms and the overall structure of the game (i.e., *consistency*). Thus, if different types pick different strategies, consumers will know with certainty which firm offers which quality. In contrast, if the two firms adopt a type-independent (pooling) strategy, consumers revert to their prior beliefs, namely that it is equally likely that either firm is the high-quality firm.

We should briefly elaborate that in the definition of equilibria we intentionally have not made any a priori distinction between the two firms. That is, if a priori we call the firms:

Firm 1 and Firm 2, we will not make any distinction between an equilibrium where Firm 1 is selected by Nature to be the high-quality firm and the case where Firm 2 is selected to be the high-quality firm. In other words, we are merely associating a strategy with a type in our definition of equilibrium. We will consider an equilibrium where the strategy of Firm 1 and Firm 2 are reversed to be the same equilibrium. That being the case, we have no reason to identify the firms prior to Nature's move.[11]

In addition, in the remainder we shall actually restrict beliefs a little further than what is immediately implied by Definition 1. Due to the ex ante symmetry of the game, we shall replace (4) in Definition 1 by:

(4') if $(p_H, A_H) = (p_L, A_L)$ then $\mu((p_H, A_H), (p_L, A_L)) = 1/2$.

Note that condition (4) refers only to price-advertising pairs on a putative pooling equilibrium path, whereas (4') refers to arbitrary pairs of identical observations. Strictly speaking, an equilibrium only requires that out-of-equilibrium beliefs satisfy (5) (i.e., summing to one), but we shall maintain the ancillary hypothesis that consumers infer no information from two identical observations, and that beliefs, therefore, stay at the priors following such observations. Thus, whenever reference is made to equilibrium in the following, (4') is implied.

Having presented our basic notion of equilibrium, we can proceed to the analysis, while refinements are studied in the next section. We start by presenting necessary conditions for the observed price-advertising pairs to constitute a separating profile.

---

[11] Thus, we restrict attention to "symmetric" equilibria. In other words, the labelling of the firms is assumed to be irrelevant. Since by design the firms are ex ante symmetric (i.e., Nature flips a fair coin), this seems reasonable. Of course, based purely on first principles we cannot rule out that consumers might be prejudiced against a firm with a particular label, and have to *impose* symmetry as an ancillary assumption. Therefore, our basic notion of equilibrium imposes more restrictions than sequential equilibrium, and although it is certainly a sequential equilibrium, we shall not refer to it as such in the characterization below.

Lemma 1: Necessary conditions for $(\hat{p}_L, \hat{A}_L) \neq (\hat{p}_H, \hat{A}_H)$ to be a separating profile are:

(1) $\Pi_L(\hat{p}_L, \hat{p}_H, \hat{A}_L, 0, L) \geq \Pi_L(\hat{p}_H, \hat{p}_H, \hat{A}_H, 1/2, L)$

(2) $\Pi_H(\hat{p}_H, \hat{p}_L, \hat{A}_H, 1, L) \geq \Pi_H(\hat{p}_L, \hat{p}_L, \hat{A}_L, 1/2, L)$

(3) $(\hat{p}_L, \hat{A}_L) \in argmax\ \Pi_L((p_L, \hat{p}_H, A_L, 0, L)$ with $(p_L, A_L) \in [0,1] \times \mathfrak{R}_+$

The three requirements are almost standard. Conditions (1) and (2) are implied by (1), (2) and (4') of the definition of an equilibrium. That is, by the construction of our belief system (under identical strategies consumer revert to their prior beliefs), mimicking the strategy of the other firm and confusing consumers is always a possibility open to each firm. Conditions (1) and (2) merely state that each firm prefers the putative separating profile to the option of mimicking the strategy of the rival firm. Finally, under a separating equilibrium, the low-quality firm faces the worst possible consumer beliefs. That being the case, altering its strategy cannot result in any less favorable beliefs. Therefore, the low-quality firm will only select a strategy that maximizes its profits, subject to this belief. This establishes condition (3). It should also be clear that in any separating equilibrium the low-quality firm would not advertise, since advertising has no direct effect on demand. We state this as part of Lemma 2.

Lemma 2: In any separating equilibrium profile $\{(\hat{p}_L, \hat{A}_L), (\hat{p}_H, \hat{A}_H)\}$, the strategy of the low-quality firm is $S_L = ((L/2)\hat{p}_H, 0)$.

Proof: Rewrite condition (3) from Lemma 1 to obtain

$$\Pi_L(p_L, \hat{p}_H, A_L, 0, L) = p_L \left(\frac{\hat{p}_H - p_L}{1-L} - \frac{p_L}{L} \right) - A_L.$$

Maximizing with respect to p_L and A_L yields the result. Q.e.d.

For later reference we now characterize the unique equilibrium of the complete information benchmark.

Proposition 1: Under complete information the equilibrium strategies and profits are:

$$S_H^* = (p_H^*, A_H^*) = \left(\frac{2(1-L)}{4-L}, 0\right) \quad S_L^* = (p_L^*, A_L^*) = \left(\frac{L(1-L)}{(4-L)}, 0\right)$$

$$\Pi_H^* = \frac{4(1-L)}{(4-L)^2} \qquad\qquad \Pi_L^* = \frac{L(1-L)}{(4-L)^2}$$

Proof: Lemma 2 gives the best response, S_L, of the low-quality firm holding fixed the beliefs of consumers. Similarly, maximizing $p_H D_H^H(p_H, \hat{p}_L, L) - A_H$ with respect to p_H and A_H yields the best response of the high-quality firm: $S_H = ((1-L)/2 + (\hat{p}_L/2), 0)$. Solving for the fixed-point of the best responses gives the complete information Nash equilibrium of the vertically differentiated duopoly game. Q.e.d.

Next, we establish that, contrary to what is the case in many two-player signaling games studied in the literature (e.g. the Spence-game in Cho and Kreps (1987)), the complete information strategies can never form an equilibrium in the present game.

Proposition 2: The complete information strategies S_L^* and S_H^* cannot constitute an equilibrium in the game with incomplete information.

Proof: By adopting the strategy $S_L^0 = (p_H^*, 0)$, the low-quality firm can achieve the following profits:

$$\Pi_L^0 = \Pi_L(p_H^*, p_H^*, 0, 1/2, L) = (1/2)(p_H^*) D_L^0(p_H^*, p_H^*, L) = (1/2)(p_H^*)\left(1 - \frac{2 p_H^*}{1+L}\right)$$

Substituting in for p_H^* gives

$$\Pi_L^0 = \left(4 - L - \frac{4(1-L)}{1+L}\right)\left(\frac{1-L}{(4-L)^2}\right).$$

Comparing this expression with Π_L^* reveals that $\Pi_L^0 > \Pi_L^*$ if and only if $4 - L - \frac{4(1-L)}{1+L} > L$, which reduces to $(6-2L)L > 0$. However, since we have already assumed that $H = 1 > L > 0$, the proposition is established. Q.e.d.

From the results above it is clear that in order for a strategy of the high-quality firm to be part of a separating equilibrium, it must be too costly for the low-quality firm to mimic. That is, the best response of the low-quality firm must be to play the strategy $S_L = ((L/2)\hat{p}_H, 0)$, instead of mimicking the strategy of the high-quality firm. Such a strategy of the high-quality firm could involve selecting an advertising expenditure that is too costly for the low-quality firm to mimic or selecting a price different from the complete information price p_H^* or some combination of the two.

Consider condition (1) of Lemma 1. Substituting in for $\hat{p}_L$ and $\hat{A}_L$ using Lemma 2 we have:

$$\Pi_L(\,(L/2)\hat{p}_H, \hat{p}_H, 0, 0, L) \geq \Pi_L(\hat{p}_H, \hat{p}_H, \hat{A}_H, 1/2, L)$$

which we can write as

$$\frac{L}{2}\hat{p}_H\left(\frac{\hat{p}_H - (L/2)\hat{p}_H}{1-L}\right) \geq (1/2)\hat{p}_H\left(1 - \frac{2\hat{p}_H}{1+L}\right) - \hat{A}_H \tag{3.1}$$

Condition (3.1) constitutes the no mimicking constraint that must be satisfied in order to deter mimicry by the low-quality firm. It should be clear that (3.1) with an equality defines a locus of price-advertising pairs. We can explicitly solve for $\hat{p}_H$ or $\hat{A}_H$ as a function of the other, and for later reference we shall do both. (3.1) reduces to:

$$\hat{A}_H \geq \overline{A}_H(\hat{p}_H) \equiv 1/2\,\hat{p}_H - \frac{4(1-L)+L(1+L)}{4(1-L^2)}\,(\hat{p}_H)^2$$

Instead, we can give the conditions on $\hat{p}_H$ as a function of $\hat{A}_H$,

$$\hat{p}_H \geq \overline{p}_{H,+}(\hat{A}_H) \equiv \frac{1-L^2}{4(1-L)+L(1+L)}\left[1 + \sqrt{1 - \frac{4(4(1-L)+L(1+L))}{1-L^2}\hat{A}_H}\,\right]$$

or $\hat{p}_H \leq \overline{p}_{H,-}(\hat{A}_H)$ (just replace "+" with "−" in the bracketed term to reflect the alternative solution to the quadratic). Combining the two conditions implies $\hat{p}_H \notin (\overline{p}_{H,-}(\hat{A}_H), \overline{p}_{H,+}(\hat{A}_H))$.

Next consider condition (2) of Lemma 1. Substituting in for $\hat{p}_L$ and $\hat{A}_L$ using Lemma 2 again we have:

15

$$\Pi_H(\hat{p}_H, (L/2)\hat{p}_H, \hat{A}_H, 1, L) \geq \Pi_H((L/2)\hat{p}_H, (L/2)\hat{p}_H, 0, 1/2, L)$$

which reduces to

$$\hat{p}_H\left(1 - \frac{\hat{p}_H - (L/2)\hat{p}_H}{1-L}\right) - \hat{A}_H \geq 1/2\,(L/2)\,\hat{p}_H\left(1 - \frac{2(L/2)\hat{p}_H}{1+L}\right). \quad (3.2)$$

Condition (3.2) constitutes the no mimicking constraint that must be satisfied in order to deter the high-quality firm from mimicking the strategy of the low-quality firm. With an equality (3.2) defines a locus of price-advertising pairs, and we can explicitly solve for $\hat{p}_H$ or $\hat{A}_H$ as a function of the other:

$$\hat{A}_H \leq \overline{\overline{A}}_H(\hat{p}_H) \equiv \left(\frac{4-L}{4}\right)\hat{p}_H - \left(\frac{2(2-L)(1+L) - L^2(1-L)}{4(1-L^2)}\right)\hat{p}_H^2.$$

We can alternatively express price as a function of advertising levels:

$$\overline{\overline{p}}_{H,\pm}(\hat{A}_H) \equiv \frac{(4-L)(1-L^2)}{2[2(2-L)(1+L) - L^2(1-L)]}\left[1 \pm \sqrt{1 - \frac{16[2(2-L)(1+L) - L^2(1-L)]\hat{A}_H}{(4-L)^2(1-L^2)}}\right]$$

Then, the joint condition is $\hat{p}_H \in [\overline{\overline{p}}_{H,-}(\hat{A}_H), \overline{\overline{p}}_{H,+}(\hat{A}_H)]$. To express the necessary conditions in a more compact form, we define two subsets of the admissible space of price and advertising.

Definition 2:
$$\mathcal{L}^S(L) = \{(p,A) : A \geq 0, A \geq \overline{A}_H(p)\} \qquad H^S(L) \equiv \{(p,A) : A \geq 0, A \leq \overline{\overline{A}}_H(p)\}$$

The requirements of Lemma 1 and Lemma 2 can now be simplified using Definition 2. In particular, the strategy of the high-quality firm must be in the intersection of $H^S(L)$ and $\mathcal{L}^S(L)$. This ensures that neither the high-quality firm nor the low-quality firm will have an incentive to mimic the strategy of its rival.

Lemma 3: Necessary conditions for $\{(\hat{p}_H, \hat{A}_H), (\hat{p}_L, \hat{A}_L)\}$ to be a separating profile are:

(1) $(\hat{p}_H, \hat{A}_H) \in \mathcal{L}^S(L) \cap H^S(L)$ \qquad (2) $(\hat{p}_L, \hat{A}_L) = ((L/2)\hat{p}_H, 0)$.

As a consequence, separation is only possible if $H^s(L) \cap \mathcal{L}^s(L) \neq \{\varnothing\}$. A simple geometric argument will help to show that the intersection is non-empty. In particular, the sets $H^s(L)$ and $\mathcal{L}^s(L)$ can be graphed on the price-advertising plane. The set $H^s(L)$ consists of all the points below the curve $\overline{\overline{A}}_H(p)$, while $\mathcal{L}^s(L)$ consists of all the points above the curve $\overline{A}_H(p)$ (see Fig. 1 below). It is easy to see that $\overline{A}_H(p)$ is an inverted parabola which reaches its maximum at[12]

$$\overline{A}_m \equiv \frac{1-L^2}{4\,[4\,(1-L)\,+\,L\,(1+L)\,]} \, .$$

Similarly, it is easy to see that $\overline{\overline{A}}_H(p)$ reaches a maximum at

$$\overline{\overline{A}}_m \equiv \frac{(4-L)^2\,(1-L^2)}{16\,[2\,(2-L)\,(1+L)\,-\,L^2\,(1-L)\,]} \, .$$

Lemma 4: $H^s(L) \cap \mathcal{L}^s(L) \neq \{\varnothing\}$ for all $L \in [0,1)$.

Proof: We want to show that there exist points in the price-advertising plane that are above $\overline{A}_H(p)$ but below $\overline{\overline{A}}_H(p)$. Put differently, we wish to show that there exists a price p such that $\overline{A}_H(p) < \overline{\overline{A}}_H(p)$. This condition is obviously satisfied for small p as $\overline{\overline{A}}_H(0) = \overline{A}_H(0) = 0$ and $\overline{\overline{A}}'_H(0) - \overline{A}'_H(0) = (4-L-2)/4 > 0$. The result would also be implied if $\overline{\overline{A}}_m > \overline{A}_m$, and tedious algebraic manipulation reveals that this is true for all $L \in [0,1)$. Furthermore, $\overline{A}_m = \overline{\overline{A}}_m$ when $L=1$. Q.e.d.

We are now ready to give our main result on separating equilibrium profiles.

Theorem 1: For all $L \in [0,1)$ any pair of strategies such that $(\hat{p}_H, \hat{A}_H) \in H^s(L) \cap \mathcal{L}^s(L)$ and $(\hat{p}_L, \hat{A}_L) = ((L/2)\,\hat{p}_H, 0)$ can be paired with a system of beliefs to form a separating equilibrium.

Proof: see appendix.

Turning to pooling equilibria, we introduce a further piece of notation.

Definition 3: $\mathcal{L}^p(L) \equiv \{(p,A) : A \geq 0, \, A \leq \overline{A}_H(p)\}$

---

[12] Take the derivative with respect to price, set equal to zero, solve for the price, and substitute back in.

Notice that $\mathcal{L}^P(L)$ is nothing but the closure of the complement of $\mathcal{L}^S(L)$. Thus, it should be obvious that $(p,A) \in \mathcal{L}^P(L)$ is a necessary condition for pooling. If, in contrast, (p,A) is in the interior of $\mathcal{L}^S(L)$, then (by construction) the low-quality firm would not wish to mimic this strategy even if it were believed to be a firm of quality ρ. We can state the following result on pooling equilibria.

Theorem 2: For all $L \in [0,1)$ any pair of strategies such that $S_H = S_L = (\hat{p}, \hat{A}) \in \mathcal{L}^P(L)$ can be paired with a system of beliefs to form a pooling equilibrium.

Proof: see appendix.

We end this section by further characterizing the set of equilibria. In particular, we wish to show the significance of the introduction of advertising. One way in which the introduction of advertising is significant is that it permits separating equilibria to exist for all possible values of L. This is evident from the following theorem, which demonstrates the non-existence of pure price separating equilibria when the degree of vertical differentiation is sufficiently small.

Theorem 3: There exist separating equilibria of the form $S_H = (\hat{p}_H, 0)$ and $S_L = ((L/2)\hat{p}_H, 0)$ if and only if $L \leq L^* \approx .6042$.

Proof: see appendix.

We can now characterize the complete set of separating and pooling equilibria. For each value of L, one needs to examine the two functions $\bar{A}_H(p)$, and $\bar{\bar{A}}_H(p)$. As shown in the proof of Lemma 4, the latter has a higher maximum value than the former, and any price-advertising pair $(\hat{p}_H, \hat{A}_H)$ between the two in the admissible space $[0,1] \times \mathfrak{R}_+$ constitutes a separating equilibrium strategy of the high-quality firm. The corresponding equilibrium strategy of the low-quality firm lies on the price axis as represented by $((L/2)\hat{p}_H, 0)$. A closer examination reveals that both functions intersect the origin where $\bar{\bar{A}}_H(p)$ has a greater slope than $\bar{A}_H(p)$. Whether they intersect again to the right of the origin depends on the value of L. When $L < L^*$, $\bar{A}_H(p)$ intersects the price axis at a lower price than $\bar{\bar{A}}_H(p)$. The interval on the price axis between the two curves represent pure price separating equilibria (i.e., no advertising by the high-quality firm). When $L = L^*$, the two curves intersect the price axis at the same price, and there exists a unique pure price separating equilibrium. On the other hand, if $L > L^*$, then $\overline{\overline{A}}_H(P)$ intersects the price axis at a lower price than $\overline{A}_H(P)$. In this case all separating equilibria must involve advertising by the high-quality firm. Finally, any price-advertising pair between the price axis and $\overline{A}_H(p)$ represents a pooling equilibrium. The three cases are illustrated in Figure 1.

[Figure 1, about here]

4. Equilibrium Refinements

In Section 3 we concluded that there will typically exist a multiplicity of both separating and pooling equilibria in the game. In this sense our results are not different from those of the large literature on monopoly signaling games. Faced with such a multiplicity, appeal is usually made to a series of well-known refinements of the equilibrium concept (see Cho and Kreps (1987) and Cho and Sobel (1990) for a synthesis). However, in the present context these refinements are of little immediate use. In Hertzendorf and Overgaard (1998) the problems are discussed at length. Suffice it to note here that an important distinguishing feature of the game considered in the present paper is that the uninformed party (the consumers) receives *two* messages[13] from the competing informed parties (the firms), whereas usually the uninformed party receives just *one* message from a single informed party. On the one hand, this implies that equilibrium refinements defined for two-player games clearly do not apply without substantial modification. As argued in Hertzendorf and Overgaard (1998), it is far from clear how existing concepts could be modified to encompass multi-sender signaling games. On the other hand, the fact that the uninformed party receives two signals may actually facilitate the inferences of the uninformed party following observed deviations from a putative profile. To illustrate this, first suppose that the putative profile under scrutiny is $((\hat{p}_H, \hat{A}_H), (\hat{p}_L, \hat{A}_L))$, where $(\hat{p}_H, \hat{A}_H) \neq (\hat{p}_L, \hat{A}_L)$.[14] That is, we consider a separating profile. Now, if consumers (unexpectedly) observe $((p^0, A^0), (\hat{p}_L, \hat{A}_L))$ where $(p^0, A^0) \notin \{(\hat{p}_H, \hat{A}_H), (\hat{p}_L, \hat{A}_L)\}$, then we might argue that consumers should *continue* to believe that $(\hat{p}_L, \hat{A}_L)$ was sent by the low-quality firm, whereas the high-quality firm has deviated to (p^0, A^0). Such out-of-equilibrium beliefs are consistent with a reconstruction (see Kreps and Wilson (1982)) of play that puts *all* probability on a history with *one* deviation from the putative profile and *no* probability on a history with *two* deviations (which is the only other reconstruction consistent with the actual observation of play). This type of argument forms the basis of refinement of separating equilibria in Bagwell and Ramey

---

[13] In fact, two pairs of price and advertising messages.

[14] Hence, $\mu((\hat{p}_H, \hat{A}_H), (\hat{p}_L, \hat{A}_L)) = 1$ and $\mu((\hat{p}_L, \hat{A}_L), (\hat{p}_H, \hat{A}_H)) = 0$.

(1991)[15], Schultz (1996) and Hertzendorf and Overgaard (1998), and shall follow this approach below when we scrutinize the set of separating equilibria from Section 3. Suppose next that the profile under consideration is $((\hat{p}_H, \hat{A}_H), (\hat{p}_L, \hat{A}_L))$ where $(\hat{p}_L, \hat{A}_L) = (\hat{p}_H, \hat{A}_H) = (\hat{p}, \hat{A})$.[16] That is, a pooling profile. If consumers unexpectedly observe $((\hat{p}, \hat{A}), (p^0, A^0))$ where $(p^0, A^0) \neq (\hat{p}, \hat{A})$, then the observation is only consistent with a single deviation from the putative profile. Given the symmetry of the objective functions of the two firms, it might be argued that consumers should be rather confused by the observation. In Section 3 we characterized the full set of sequential pooling equilibria by positing pessimistic beliefs following single deviations, that is, $\mu((p^0, A^0), (\hat{p}, \hat{A})) = 0$. Given the coincidence of firm incentives, below we require $\mu((p^0, A^0), (\hat{p}, \hat{A})) = 1/2$ to capture the ex post confusion of consumers, and we show how this dramatically reduces the set of pooling equilibrium profiles. In fact, the set reduces to a single point, which basically constitutes a standard zero-profit Bertrand equilibrium.

4.1 Separating Equilibria

We now take a closer look at the set of separating profiles characterized in Theorem 4. Consumers expect to observe $((\hat{p}_H, \hat{A}_H), (\hat{p}_L, \hat{A}_L))$, where $(\hat{p}_H, \hat{A}_H) \neq (\hat{p}_L, \hat{A}_L)$, with associated beliefs $\mu((\hat{p}_H, \hat{A}_H), (\hat{p}_L, \hat{A}_L)) = 1$. Furthermore, recall that $(\hat{p}_H, \hat{A}_H) \in \mathcal{L}^S(L) \cap H^S(L)$ and $(\hat{p}_L, \hat{A}_L) = ((L/2)\hat{p}_H, 0)$. Note before we continue that, by the requirements of equilibrium, the low-quality firm is playing a best response to $(\hat{p}_H, \hat{A}_H)$, and the high-quality firm is playing a best response to $(\hat{p}_L, \hat{A}_L)$. Best responses are predicated on an admissible system of beliefs as explained in Section 3. Below we want to scrutinize the pessimistic beliefs specified in the previous section following observations consistent with a single deviation. In Section 3 we required (to span the equilibrium set of Theorem 1) that $((p^0, A^0), (\hat{p}_L, \hat{A}_L))$ with $(p^0, A^0) \notin \{(\hat{p}_H, \hat{A}_H), (\hat{p}_L, \hat{A}_L)\}$, be followed by the beliefs $\mu((p^0, A^0), (\hat{p}_L, \hat{A}_L)) = 0$. Effectively, this requires consumers to put *all* probability weight on the consistent reconstruction of play

---

[15] Bagwell and Ramey (1991) introduced the notion of unprejudiced beliefs.

[16] Consequently, $\mu((\hat{p}_H, \hat{A}_H), (\hat{p}_L, \hat{A}_L)) = \mu((\hat{p}_L, \hat{A}_L), (\hat{p}_H, \hat{A}_H)) = \mu((\hat{p}, \hat{A}), (\hat{p}, \hat{A})) = 1/2$.

involving *two* simultaneous deviations from the putative profile $((\hat{p}_H, \hat{A}_H), (\hat{p}_L, \hat{A}_L))$ and *no* weight on the alternative (consistent) reconstruction involving *one* deviation. In other words, prior to the observations (ex ante) consumers expect the high-quality firm to choose $(\hat{p}_H, \hat{A}_H)$ with probability one and the low-quality firm to choose $(\hat{p}_L, \hat{A}_L)$ with probability one. Then $((p^0, A^0), (\hat{p}_L, \hat{A}_L))$ is observed, and subsequently (ex post) consumers believe that the low-quality firm chose (p^0, A^0) with probability one, while the high-quality firm chose $(\hat{p}_L, \hat{A}_L)$ with probability one. No weight is attached to the possibility that the low-quality firm has stuck to its part of the putative profile, while the high-quality firm has deviated to (p^0, A^0).

Absent a possibility of correlated deviations, these out-of-equilibrium beliefs seem implausible. To remedy this, we shall propose an alternative that concentrates probability weight on reconstructions consistent with a *minimal* number of deviations from the putative profile.[17] To set the scene, consider a profile $((\hat{p}_H, \hat{A}_H), (\hat{p}_L, \hat{A}_L))$ from the set of separating equilibrium profiles characterized in Theorem 4. Take any alternative profile $((p^i, A^i), (p^j, A^j)) \neq ((\hat{p}_H, \hat{A}_H), (\hat{p}_L, \hat{A}_L))$, where $(p^i, A^i) \neq (p^j, A^j)$,[18] then we require the following:

Definition 4: REDE (Resistance to Equilibrium Defections) An equilibrium profile $((\hat{p}_H, \hat{A}_H), (\hat{p}_L, \hat{A}_L))$ is resistant to equilibrium defections if beliefs satisfy $\mu((p^i, A^i), (p^j, A^j)) = 1$ whenever

(1) $(p^i, A^i) \in \mathcal{L}^S(L) \cap H^S(L)$, and
(2) $(p^j, A^j) = ((L/2)\tilde{p}, 0)$ for some $(\tilde{p}, \tilde{A}) \in \mathcal{L}^S(L) \cap H^S(L)$

Although REDE is defined quite generally, it is only an equilibrium refinement to the extent it restricts *out-of-equilibrium* beliefs. The heuristic content of REDE is roughly as follows. Consumers expect $(\hat{p}_H, \hat{A}_H)$ and $(\hat{p}_L, \hat{A}_L)$ from the high-quality and the low-quality firms, respectively. Instead they observe $((p^i, A^i), (p^j, A^j))$. If (p^i, A^i), say, is consistent with some alternative separating equilibrium play by the high-quality firm, and (p^j, A^j) is consistent with some (not necessarily the same)

---

[17] For a more formal discussion of consistent reconstructions of play, the reader is referred to Bagwell and Ramey (1991), and Hertzendorf and Overgaard (1998).

[18] If $(p^i, A^i) = (p^j, A^j)$, our previous assumptions already imply that $\mu((p^i, A^i), (p^j, A^j)) = 1/2$.

separating equilibrium play of the low-quality firm, then consumers believe with probability one that (p^i, A^i) was played by the high-quality firm, and (p^j, A^j) was played by the low-quality firm. This is the sense in which beliefs are resistant to defections to alternative equilibrium pairs. Thus, it is as if consumers consider the actual observations (partly) in isolation and ask whether they are consistent with the two firms playing for separating equilibrium.

Of course, this interpretation is only sensible if the sets of potential separating equilibrium strategies for the low-quality firm and high-quality firm are disjoint. Since, the low-quality firm would never choose positive advertising in a separating equilibrium, the two sets are obviously disjoint if the pure price separating equilibrium strategies also fail to overlap. This is clearly the case as $(L/2)\overline{\overline{p}}_{H,+}(0) < \overline{p}_{H,+}(0)$. That is, the highest price that the low-quality firm would ever charge in a pure price separating equilibrium is less than the lowest price that the high-quality firm would ever charge in such an equilibrium. (see Hertzendorf and Overgaard (1998)).

Since firms are assumed unable to engineer correlated defections, the crucial special case of REDE follows observations of the type $((p^i, A^i), (p^j, A^j))$, where $(p^i, A^i) \notin \{(\hat{p}_H, \hat{A}_H), (\hat{p}_L, \hat{A}_L)\}$ and $(p^i, A^i) \in \{(\hat{p}_H, \hat{A}_H), (\hat{p}_L, \hat{A}_L)\}$, i.e. when one part of the putative profile is not observed, while the other is. Then REDE requires that beliefs be robust as long as the (unexpected) observation of (p^i, A^i) is consistent with some alternative separating equilibrium for type $t' \neq t$ given that $(\hat{p}_t, \hat{A}_t)$ is also observed. In particular, any observation $((p^i, A^i), (\hat{p}_L, \hat{A}_L))$ with $(p^i, A^i) \in \mathcal{L}^S(L) \cap H^S(L)$ is followed by the beliefs $\mu((p^i, A^i), (\hat{p}_L, \hat{A}_L)) = 1$. This illustrates the sense in which REDE concentrates all probability weight on reconstructions consistent with a minimal number of deviations.

Let us turn to the implications of imposing REDE. To span the set of separating profiles that survives the imposition of REDE we continue to specify pessimistic beliefs whenever REDE is silent. In particular, $\mu((p^i, A^i), (\hat{p}_L, \hat{A}_L)) = 0$ for all $(p^i, A^i) \notin \mathcal{L}^S(L) \cap H^S(L)$.

Now consider the two firms in turn. When the low-quality firm is considering unilateral defections away from the putative separating profile $((\hat{p}_L, \hat{A}_L), (\hat{p}_H, \hat{A}_H))$, the imposition of REDE has no consequences. Under REDE, $(\hat{p}_L, \hat{A}_L) = ((L/2)\hat{p}_H, 0))$ continues to be the unique best response of the low-quality firm to $S_H = (\hat{p}_H, \hat{A}_H)$. That is, we originally supported the given separating equilibrium by assuming that defections are followed by the belief that the defecting firm offers low-quality goods. From the perspective of the low-quality firm this is unchanged provided we continue to specify pessimistic beliefs for those observations on which REDE is silent. Although it is true that defections to $(\hat{p}_H, \hat{A}_H)$ by the low-quality firm result in $\mu((\hat{p}_H, \hat{A}_H), (\hat{p}_H, \hat{A}_H)) = 1/2$, the equilibrium has been constructed so that such a defection is suboptimal. Hence, we need not consider the low-quality firm any further.

In contrast, for the high-quality firm the implications of REDE are dramatic. To see this, we first note that, given REDE, unilateral deviations by the high-quality firm from $(\hat{p}_H, \hat{A}_H)$ to any other $(p^0, A^0) \in \mathcal{L}^S(L) \cap H^S(L)$ leave beliefs unaltered (i.e. $\mu((p^0, A^0), (\hat{p}_L, \hat{A}_L)) = 1 \ \forall \ (p^0, A^0) \in \mathcal{L}^S(L) \cap H^S(L)$). Further, deviations to $(p^0, A^0) \notin \mathcal{L}^S(L) \cap H^S(L)$ lead to $\mu((p^0, A^0), (\hat{p}_L, \hat{A}_L)) = 0$ and will not be contemplated by the high-quality firm (i.e., these are the same pessimistic beliefs we originally assumed to support the given equilibrium). The upshot of this is that for $((\hat{p}_H, \hat{A}_H), (\hat{p}_L, \hat{A}_L))$ to survive the imposition of REDE, $(\hat{p}_H, \hat{A}_H)$ must be a best response to $(\hat{p}_L, \hat{A}_L) = ((L/2)\hat{p}_H, 0)$ on the set $\mathcal{L}^S(L) \cap H^S(L)$. If not, sequential rationality requires the high-quality firm to deviate, and the profile $((\hat{p}_H, \hat{A}_H), (\hat{p}_L, \hat{A}_L))$ is destabilized.

We want to show that the imposition of REDE destabilizes all but one separating profile. To this end we need a final piece of notation. Fix a separating profile, $(\hat{p}_H, \hat{A}_H) = (p, \hat{A}_H)$, $(\hat{p}_L, \hat{A}_L) = ((L/2)p, 0)$. If the no-mimicking constraint is binding, i.e., $\hat{A}_H = \Pi_L(p, p, 0, 1/2, L) - \Pi_L(\hat{p}_L, p, 0, 0, L)$, then we can write the equilibrium payoffs of the high-quality firm, $\Pi_H(p, \hat{p}_L, \hat{A}_H, 1, L)$ as a function of p and $\hat{p}_L$,

$$\bar{\Pi}_H(p; \hat{p}_L) = \Pi_H(p, \hat{p}_L, 0, 1, L) - [\Pi_L(p, p, 0, 1/2, L) - \Pi_L(\hat{p}_L, p, 0, 0, L)] \quad (4.1)$$

where the bracketed term is the advertising expenditure. Finally, let $\tilde{p}_H(L)$ be the solution to

$$\frac{d\bar{\Pi}_H(p; (L/2)p)}{dp} = 0.$$ Then, $\tilde{p}_H(L) = (1 - L^2)/(2L(3 - L))$. Now, we can

state our main result on separating equilibria.

24

Theorem 4: With any $L \in (0,1)$ is associated a unique separating equilibrium profile which survives REDE.[19]

i) If $L \geq L^{**}$, then $(\hat{p}_H, \hat{A}_H) = (\tilde{p}_H(L), \overline{A}_H(\tilde{p}_H(L)))$, $(\hat{p}_L, \hat{A}_L) = ((L/2)\tilde{p}_H(L), 0)$

ii) If $L \leq L^{**}$, then $(\hat{p}_H, \hat{A}_H) = (\overline{p}_{H,+}(0), 0)$, $(\hat{p}_L, \hat{A}_L) = ((L/2)\overline{p}_{H,+}(0), 0)$

Proof: see appendix.

Theorem 4 has a simple and intuitive interpretation. In the following discussion we illustrate how all but one putative separating equilibrium will fail to satisfy REDE. In particular, we show how the high-quality firm can exploit the beliefs implied by REDE to increase its profits. For the moment we hold fixed the strategy the of the low-quality firm and consider putative separating equilibria that involve a strictly positive level of advertising. In the appendix (Lemma 5) we first show that under REDE the high-quality firm would never choose to sink more resources into signaling than is necessary. Hence, if the high-quality firm is maximizing its profits, it must adopt a strategy of the form $S_H = (p, \overline{A}_H(p))$, and any adopted signaling strategy with advertising must lie on the curve $\overline{A}_H(p)$. Some insight into Theorem 4 can be derived by considering the derivative of the right-hand side of (4.1) with respect to p:

$$\frac{d\Pi_H(p, \hat{p}_L, 0, 1, L)}{dp} - \left[\frac{d\Pi_L(p, p, 0, 1/2, L)}{dp} - \frac{d\Pi_L(\hat{p}_L, p, 0, 0, L)}{dp}\right]. \qquad (4.2)$$

Start at any putative separating equilibrium of the form $S_H = (p, \overline{A}_H(p))$, where $\overline{A}_H(P) > 0$, and $S_L = ((L/2)p, 0)$, and consider a small change in price by the high-quality firm. The first term represents the gain or loss in revenue to the high-quality firm associated with this change in price (holding fixed beliefs and the price of its rival). The bracketed term reflects the change in the gain in revenue that the low-quality firm would receive from mimicking *just* the price of its high-quality rival. According to REDE and our specification of out-of-equilibrium beliefs the high-quality firm must adjust its advertising expenditure by at least this amount to maintain the perception that it is a high-quality firm. (Such an adjustment would result in a new strategy

---

[19] For later reference $L^{**} \equiv 0.2958 < L^* \equiv 0.6042$.

consistent with an alternative separating equilibrium strategy for the high-quality firm and according to REDE leaves beliefs unaffected.) However, according to Lemma 5 (see appendix) the high-quality firm must adjust its advertising expenditures exactly by this amount (and no more) to offset the altered incentives of the low-quality firm to mimic its strategy. (Note that if the bracketed term is evaluated at $\hat{p}_L=(L/2)p$, it is equivalent to $d\overline{A}_H(p)/dp$.)

Roughly speaking, the two terms in (4.2) reflect the marginal cost of signaling via price or advertising. When the expression is positive, gains in revenue associated with an increase in price more than offset any additional cost in advertising that may be necessary to deter mimicry. Similarly, when the expression is negative, the gains in revenue associated with a reduction in price more than offsets any additional cost in advertising that may be necessary to deter mimicry. If the two terms are of opposite sign, then this merely provides two incentives for the high-quality firm to adjust its price. That is, the high-quality firm can increase its revenue and reduce its advertising budget at the same time. When the high-quality firm is maximizing its profits (subject to beliefs that satisfy REDE) the expression must be equal to zero; otherwise a slight reduction or increase in price would be advantageous. Setting (4.2) equal to zero one can solve for p as a function of $\hat{p}_L$. Replacing $\hat{p}_L$ with $(L/2)p$ yields $\tilde{p}_H(L)$.

When a pure price-separating equilibrium is optimal (i.e., $L<L^{**}$) it must be the case that (4.2) evaluated at $p=\overline{p}_{H,+}(0)$ is negative. This reflects the fact that the gain in revenue associated with a reduction is price would be more than offset by the corresponding increase in advertising necessary to deter mimicry.

4.2 Pooling Equilibria

We shall provide a largely heuristic argument to slice the set of pooling equilibrium pairs in $\mathcal{L}^P(L)$. Recall that $\mathcal{L}^P(L)$ is (the closure of) the complement of $\mathcal{L}^S(L)$. It follows that the admissible price-advertising pairs are bounded by $A \leq \overline{A}_H(p)$ and $A \geq 0$. Suppose consumers expect a profile $((\hat{p}_H, \hat{A}_H), (\hat{p}_L, \hat{A}_L))$ where $(\hat{p}_H, \hat{A}_H) = (\hat{p}_L, \hat{A}_L) = (\hat{p}, \hat{A}) \in \mathcal{L}^P(L)$. In Section 3 we spanned the set by postulating (admissible) pessimistic out-of-equilibrium beliefs following all observations consistent with a unilateral deviation, that is $\mu((p,A),(\hat{p},\hat{A}))=0$ for all $(p,A) \neq (\hat{p},\hat{A})$. In other words,

26

whenever consumers observe a unilateral deviation, they conclude with certainty that the deviating player has a low quality. At the beginning of this section we argued that this interpretation of out-of-equilibrium observations is not entirely satisfactory given that both firms have exactly the same incentives to defect. Let us expand a little on this and suggest a natural alternative specification of out-of-equilibrium beliefs that has dramatic consequences for the set of sustainable pooling profiles.[20]

Recall that "coming into the game" the consumers have a diffuse prior as to the identity of the two firms. We have already used this to argue that any pair of identical choices by the firms (whether in or out of equilibrium) should be met by an equally diffuse posterior, that is, $\mu((p,A),(p,A))=1/2$ for all (p,A). In addition, consumers are assumed to know that the basic payoff functions of the two firms are identical. Now, suppose consumers expect to observe $((\hat{p},\hat{A}),(\hat{p},\hat{A}))$, but instead observe one firm choosing $(\hat{p},\hat{A})$ and the other choosing $(p,A)\neq(\hat{p},\hat{A})$. How should consumers reason? The consumers know for a fact that one firm has played its part of the putative profile, while the other has deviated to (p,A). However, given the identical incentives of the two firms there appears to be no basis for assuming that the defection came from one firm versus the other. As a consequence, it appears rather natural to suggest that consumer inference should not be affected by unilateral deviations from putative pooling profiles, and we formalize this below.

Definition 5: Payoffs are **identical at pooling profiles**, $S_H=S_L=(\hat{p},\hat{A})$, if $\Pi_H(\hat{p},\hat{p},\hat{A},\mu,L)=\Pi_L(\hat{p},\hat{p},\hat{A},\mu,L)$ and $\Pi_H(p',\hat{p},A',\mu,L)=$

$\Pi_L(p',\hat{p},A',\mu,L)$ for all admissible (p',A') and $\mu\in[0,1]$.

Definition 6: Out-of-equilibrium beliefs are **Impartial** at a pooling equilibrium $S_H=S_L=(\hat{p},\hat{A})$ if **identical payoffs** are associated with out-of-equilibrium beliefs $\mu((\hat{p},\hat{A}),(p',A'))=1/2$.

In other words, a more reasonable assumption is that consumers revert to their prior beliefs following a unilateral defection from

---

[20] For a somewhat different perspective on pooling equilibria in this type of game, we refer the reader to Hertzendorf and Overgaard (1998).

a putative pooling profile. We wish to stress that we are not arguing as a general rule of thumb that unilateral defections away from putative pooling equilibrium should have no affect on beliefs. Rather, it is the unique feature of having identical payoff functions that makes this natural in the game considered here. The implication is that at almost any pooling equilibrium each firm would have an incentive to defect. This is because defection has no impact on consumer expectations, and, by charging a slightly lower price than its rival, each firm can capture the entire market. Hence, almost all the pooling equilibria are destabilized. The one exception is the "Bertrand" pooling equilibrium where both firms earn zero profits and give their product away for free ($\hat{p}_H = \hat{p}_L = 0$).

Theorem 5: The only pooling equilibrium that is sustained by impartial out-of-equilibrium beliefs is $S_H = S_L = (0,0)$.

Proof: see appendix.

5. Discussion

In this section we summarize and further discuss the findings in Section 4. Theorems 4 and 5 leave us with two candidates for a focal outcome, if the equilibrium selection procedures of Section 4 are accepted. One outcome is separating and admits strictly positive profits to both firms, while the other is a zero-profit pooling outcome a la Bertrand despite the products being vertically differentiated.

In the following we shall concentrate our comments on the separating outcome. However, the zero-profit pooling outcome is certainly of interest in its own right, since it suggests that a high-quality duopolist may have a very hard time separating itself from a low-quality competitor, even if both price and advertising signals are available. Going somewhat beyond the present model, this type of problem suggests why an oligopolist would introduce further signals such as warranties, quality-certification, buy-back guarantees, etc. in a multiperiod setting.

Returning to the separating outcome of Theorem 4, there are a couple of noteworthy features we wish to emphasize. Figure 2 illustrates the strategies of the two firms associated with the unique separating profile. In the figure the strategies are given as functions of L as it varies from zero to one. In the special case where $L=0$, the model collapses to a standard monopoly since the low-quality product has no value to potential customers. Consequently, the high-quality firm separates by setting the standard monopoly price ($\hat{p}_H = 1/2$), as if the low-quality firm did not exist. The special case where $L=1$ corresponds to a traditional, homogenous-goods Bertrand duopoly with pricing at cost $\hat{p}_H = \hat{p}_L = 0$ and zero profits to both firms.

[**Figure 2 about here**]

For intermediate values of L, the figure illustrates how prices and the level of dissipative advertising by the high-quality firm varies in separating equilibrium as L varies (recall that the low-quality firm never advertises in a separating equilibrium). Panel (b) of Figure 2 (which just gives max $\{0, \bar{A}_H(\hat{p}_H)\}$ as a function of L) shows that the level of advertising expenditures incurred by the high-quality firm is non-monotonic in L. For values of L less than or equal to L^{**} (a large degree of vertical differentiation), advertising is not used to separate, while advertising expenditures

29

are strictly positive for L larger than L^{**}. In the latter case, $\hat{A}_H$ is initially increasing in L, attains a maximum at an interior value of L, while it naturally approaches zero as the two goods become perfect substitutes in consumption (i.e., as $L \to 1$). Thus, as an empirical matter, this model suggests that we should expect to observe advertising to be used most intensively when a high-quality firm competes against a supplier of a "moderately close" low-quality substitute, while we should not observe advertising when goods are "poor" substitutes.

A second interesting feature of our results on separating equilibria relates to the "distortion" of the prices compared to the complete information bench-mark of Proposition 1. Before proceeding we note that under complete information $p_L^* = (L/2)\, p_H^*$, while $\hat{p}_L = (L/2)\, \hat{p}_H$ in any separating equilibrium of the incomplete information game. This one-to-one relationship between the prices of the two firms immediately implies that whenever the price of the high-quality firm is distorted upwards (downwards), the price of low-quality firm is likewise distorted. This is just a manifestation of the strategic complementarity of prices in the underlying Bertrand game. Now, an immediate corollary of our results is the following.

Corollary 1: In any pure price separating equilibrium $\hat{p}_H > p_H^*$ and $\hat{p}_L > p_L^*$.

Proof: It suffices to show that $\hat{p}_H > p_H^*$. Then, absent advertising, it must be the case that $\hat{p} \in [\underline{p}_{H,+}(0), \overline{\overline{p}}_{H,+}(0)]$. Thus, on the assumption that the set is non-empty, $\hat{p}_H \geq \underline{p}_{H,+}(0)$. But using the definition of $\underline{p}_{H,+}(0)$ and p_H^*, it is easy to show that $\underline{p}_{H,+}(0) > p_H^*$ for all $L \in (0,1)$. Q.e.d.

The corollary establishes that in any pure price separating equilibrium both prices are distorted upwards. This distinguishes our results significantly from those of the literature on monopoly models of price signaling, where a representative result is that the price of the high-quality type is distorted upwards, while the price of the low-quality type is undistorted and constant across all separating equilibrium profiles.

Despite this result on pure price signaling, we know that a pure price separating equilibrium may not exist, and further that it may not survive REDE. The implication for the pricing of the high-quality firm in the unique refined separating equilibrium of our model is illustrated in Figure 3.

[Figure 3, about here]

In this figure the refined separating equilibrium price, $\hat{p}_H$, is plotted alongside the complete information price of Proposition 1 (and we note that both are, of course, functions of L). To proceed, let us define $L^{***} \equiv \{L \mid \tilde{p}_H(L) = p_H^*\}$, where $\tilde{p}_H(L)$ is defined in Section 4.[21] Then we can state our last formal result.

Corollary 2: At the unique refined separating equilibrium profile

(i) $\hat{p}_H$ and $\hat{p}_L$ are distorted upwards if $L < L^{***}$

(ii) $\hat{p}_H$ and $\hat{p}_L$ are undistorted if $L = L^{***}$

(iii) $\hat{p}_H$ and $\hat{p}_L$ are distorted downwards if $L > L^{***}$.

These results can be understood in terms of the sign of the expression in (4.2) of the previous section evaluated at $p = p_H^*$. Consider the case where $(p_H^*, \bar{A}_H(p_H^*)) \in H^s(L) \cap \mathcal{L}^s(L)$. The high-quality firm could prevent mimicry by maintaining the complete information price and supplementing it with an adequate dose of advertising. However, the imposition of REDE would destabilize such a strategy unless $L = L^{***}$. At this value of L, the expression in (4.2), evaluated at $p = p_H^*$ equals zero and there is no gain to the high-quality firm from substituting advertising signals for price signals. For smaller values of L, the high-quality firm could increase profits by reducing advertising and increasing price. While for larger values of L the reverse is true.

The most striking feature of this result is that when $L > L^{***}$ the efficient mix of signals from the point of view of the high-quality firm consists of prices that are lower than under complete information together with a strictly positive amount of dissipative advertising. That is, advertising signals have the capacity to lower prices. Thus, a main result of this paper is to contradict the naive perception that dissipative advertising expenditures necessarily imply inflated prices on the argument that advertising

---

[21] We note that $L^{***} \approx 0.5426$.

expenditures have to be "recovered" from sales to consumers.

In case the reader is confused a brief discussion of special values of L follows. First we note that $0 < L^{**} < L^{***} < L^{*}$.[22] For small values of L ($L < L^{**}$), REDE indicates that all separation occurs in price. For all larger values of L ($L > L^{**}$), REDE indicates that separation will occur utilizing both price and advertising signals. For $L \in (L^{**}, L^{*})$ pure price separation is possible according to the definition of equilibrium, but will fail to satisfy REDE. Lastly, L^{***} refers to the unique value of L at which the separating equilibrium (satisfying REDE) involves prices that coincide with the complete information prices. Thus, in the spirit of the corollary, we might say that dissipative advertising plays its most active role as a signal of high quality when the level of the low quality (i.e., "L") is in the neighborhood of L^{***}, since prices are only marginally distorted in that case.

---

[22] Recall that $L^{**} \approx 0.29584$ and $L^{*} \approx 0.6042$.

32

6. Conclusion

The purpose of this paper was to examine whether or not price and dissipative advertising signals can convey information about product quality in a competitive environment. Previous literature that deals with signaling to consumers is almost exclusively limited to the monopoly case. We have taken the next logical step by extending this literature to the case of a duopoly. In so doing, we have also extended our earlier research on ducpoly price signaling (see Hertzendorf and Overgaard (1998)). Our results confirm that in an oligopoly setting it is indeed possible for simultaneous price and advertising signals to convey information about product quality to consumers. At the same time there are interesting differences between the duopoly game and the monopoly game[23]. There are also significant differences between this research and our earlier research that focused solely on price signals.

We conclude that, unlike in the monopoly case, a separating equilibrium in the duopoly game does not depend on the high-quality and low-quality firms having different profit functions (a priori). Instead it is the equilibrium itself which differentiates the payoffs to each firm. We also showed that the complete information price will never separate the two qualities unless there are also advertising signals.

The addition of advertising to the duopoly setting is important in that it permits separation to take place for any degree of vertical product differentiation. When the differentiation is greatest, price signals are used exclusively, while when the difference in quality is less, a mixture of price and advertising signals are utilized. In our view, this conclusion comports well with empirical evidence. This contrasts to our earlier research that showed that separation was not possible when the differentiation was not sufficiently large and price was the only available signal.

The addition of advertising also complicates the nature of the correlation between price and quality. Advertising signals have a tendency to reduce distortions in price that result from signaling. When the difference in quality is sufficiently small the result is that prices are distorted below the complete information prices.

---

[23] See Hertzendorf (1990) for a simple one-period monopoly game that implements the theory of Milgrom and Roberts (1986).

At the same time, advertising is also a function of the degree of vertical product differentiation. Advertising levels peak at an intermediate level and converge to zero as the high- and low-quality products become indistinguishable. These results indicate that any empirical test of the signaling hypothesis must be carefully constructed. Advertising is not just a function of quality, but rather a (non-monotonic) function of the difference in quality between two or more competing products.

A second goal of our research was to develop an analytically tractable framework in which to study signaling in an oligopoly setting. In this respect this paper builds upon our previous research through the introduction of multiple signals. Our arguments regarding equilibrium refinement have also been refined and simplified. A goal for future research would be to apply the underlying (game theory) technology to different settings. Another goal would be to study the case of an arbitrary number of firms instead of two.

Appendix

Proof of Theorem 1: We need to check that neither the low-quality nor the high-quality firm has an incentive to deviate from its respective strategy, given an appropriate specification of out-of-equilibrium beliefs.

Define out-of-equilibrium beliefs such that $\mu((\hat{p}_H, \hat{A}_H), (p, A)) = 1$ for all $(p, A) \notin \{(\hat{p}_L, \hat{A}_L), (\hat{p}_H, \hat{A}_H)\}$ and such that $\mu((p, A), (\hat{p}_L, \hat{A}_L)) = 0$ for all $(p, A) \notin \{(\hat{p}_L, \hat{A}_L), (\hat{p}_H, \hat{A}_H)\}$. These are the beliefs that can support the widest possible set of equilibria. Intuitively, these beliefs specify that any defecting firm is viewed as offering a low-quality product. This creates the greatest possible disincentive for defection.

It is easy to check that the low-quality firm has no incentive to deviate. Any deviation to $(p, A) \neq (\hat{p}_H, \hat{A}_H)$ leaves beliefs unaffected. Since by construction the low-quality firm is already maximizing its profits subject to these beliefs, such a defection must be suboptimal. A deviation to $(p, A) = (\hat{p}_H, \hat{A}_H)$ implies that $\mu((\hat{p}_H, \hat{A}_H), (\hat{p}_H, \hat{A}_H)) = 1/2$ by the definition of a equilibrium. However, since by construction $(\hat{p}_H, \hat{A}_H) \in \mathcal{L}^S(L)$ such a defection will also be suboptimal.

Showing that the high-quality firm has no incentive to deviate is a bit more complicated, and we do so in three steps. First, we note that any deviation by the high-quality firm to (p, A) where $p > \hat{p}_L$ results in zero demand, since the rival then has a lower price and will then be believed to offer high quality. Since profits are positive in equilibrium such a defection must be suboptimal.

Second, we note that a deviation by the high-quality firm to $(\hat{p}_L, \hat{A}_L)$ implies that $\mu((\hat{p}_L, \hat{A}_L), (\hat{p}_L, \hat{A}_L)) = 1/2$. However, since by construction $(\hat{p}_H, \hat{A}_H) \in H^S(L)$ such a defection is (at least weakly) dominated by the putative equilibrium strategy $S_H = (\hat{p}_H, \hat{A}_H)$.

This leaves deviations by the high-quality firm to a strategy (p, A) such that $p < \hat{p}_L$. Since any deviation by the high-quality firm implies that $\mu((p, A), (\hat{p}_L, \hat{A}_L)) = 0$, it should be clear that the optimal such defection (of this type) will not involve advertising. The demand facing the high-quality firm, when believed to offer low-quality (and charging the lower price) is

$$D_H^L(p, \hat{p}_L, L) = \frac{\hat{p}_L - p}{1 - L} - \frac{p}{L}$$

and the payoff is $p D_H^L(p, \hat{p}_L, L) = p \left(\dfrac{\hat{p}_L - p}{1-L} - \dfrac{p}{L} \right)$.

Maximizing with respect to p gives $p = (L/2) \hat{p}_L$. But recall that $\hat{p}_L = (L/2) \hat{p}_H$. We concluded that $p = (L^2/4) \hat{p}_H$ is the best deviation that involves setting a price below that set by the low-quality firm. We now wish to show that the high-quality firm can never have an incentive to deviate to $S_H' = ((L^2/4) \hat{p}_H, 0)$ from the initial putative equilibrium $S_H = (\hat{p}_H, \hat{A}_H)$. This would then imply the same for all similar such defections. The equilibrium profits resulting from this defection are

$$\Pi_H(p, \hat{p}_L, 0, 0, L) = \frac{L^3}{16 (1-L)} (\hat{p}_H)^2$$

Now it is impossible to determine exactly what profits result from the putative equilibrium strategy $S_H = (\hat{p}_H, \hat{A}_H)$ since we have not yet indicated a unique putative equilibrium. Nevertheless, we know that since $S_H \in H^S(L)$ it must be the case that

$$\Pi_H(\hat{p}_H, (L/2) \hat{p}_H, \hat{A}_H, 1, L) \geq \Pi_H((L/2) \hat{p}_H, (L/2) \hat{p}_H, 0, 1/2, L)$$

Hence, we are done if we can show that

$$\Pi((L^2/4) \hat{p}_H, (L/2) \hat{p}_H, 0, 0, L) < \Pi((L/2) \hat{p}_H, (L/2) \hat{p}_H, 0, 1/2, L).$$

Rewriting this last inequality, we are trying to show that

$$\frac{L^3 (\hat{p}_H)^2}{16 (1-L)} < \frac{L \hat{p}_H}{4} \left(1 - \frac{L \hat{p}_H}{1+L} \right).$$

Some more algebraic manipulation implies:

$$(1+L) (L^2) \hat{p}_H < (4) (1-L) (1 + L - L \hat{p}_H).$$

This last inequality is true if $\hat{p}_H < \dfrac{4 (1-L^2)}{L(L^2 - 3L + 4)}$.

However, by construction we know that $\hat{p}_H \leq \overline{\overline{p}}_{H,+}(\hat{A}_H)$ and by examining the formula we can see that $\overline{\overline{p}}_{H,+}(\hat{A}_H)$ reaches a maximum when $\hat{A}_H = 0$. We are therefore done if we can show that

36

$$\bar{\bar{p}}_{H,+}(0) = \frac{2(4-L)(1-L^2)}{4(2-L)(1+L)-2L^2(1-L)} < \frac{4(1-L^2)}{L(L^2-3L+4)}.$$

That is, if we can show that the requirement $(\hat{p}_H, \hat{A}_H) \in H^s(L)$ already implies the inequality we require to be true. This last inequality would be true if

$$\frac{1}{4+2L-L^2+L^3} < \frac{1}{L^3-3L^2+4L}$$

Since both sides are positive this last inequality is equivalent to $4+2L>4L$ or $4>2L$, and this is obviously true for all $L \in [0,1]$. Q.e.d.

Proof of Theorem 2: As in the previous theorem we need to check that neither firm has an incentive to deviate from its respective strategy, given an appropriate specification of out-of-equilibrium beliefs.

Define out-of-equilibrium beliefs such that $\mu((p,A),(\hat{p},\hat{A})) = 0$ for all $(p,A) \neq (\hat{p},\hat{A})$. These are the beliefs that can support the widest possible set of equilibria. Intuitively, these beliefs specify that any defecting firm is viewed as offering a low-quality product. This creates the greatest possible disincentive for defection.

We need to compare the potential profits from defecting to profits that result from the putative pooling equilibrium. A defecting firm faces the profit function

$$\Pi(p,\hat{p},\hat{A},0,L) = p\left(\frac{\hat{p}-p}{1-L}-\frac{p}{L}\right) - A.$$

Maximization with respect to p and A reveals that the optimal such defection is to the strategy $(p,A) = ((L/2)p,0)$. Substituting this back into the profit function reveals that the best possible profits from defecting are

$$\Pi((L/2)\hat{p},\hat{p},0,0,L) = \frac{(L)(\hat{p})^2}{4(1-L)}.$$

On the other hand, the profits from the putative pooling equilibrium are

$$\Pi(\hat{p},\hat{p},\hat{A},1/2,L) = \frac{\hat{p}}{2}\left(1-\frac{2\hat{p}}{1+L}\right) - \hat{A}.$$

37

The condition $\Pi(\hat{p}, \hat{p}, \hat{A}, 1/2, L) - \hat{A} \geq \Pi((L/2)\hat{p}, \hat{p}, 0, 0, L)$ reduces to

$$0 \leq \hat{A} \leq \frac{\hat{p}}{2} - \left(\frac{4(1-L) + L(1+L)}{4(1-L^2)} \right)(\hat{p})^2 \equiv \overline{A}_H(\hat{p}).$$

This is equivalent to requiring that $(\hat{p}, \hat{A}) \in \mathcal{L}^P(L)$. QED.

Proof of Theorem 3: This is just a special case of Theorem 1. In particular, we wish to find $(p, 0) \in H^S(L) \cap \mathcal{L}^S(L)$. This condition is equivalent to finding a $\overline{p}_{H,+}(0) \leq p \leq \overline{\overline{p}}_{H,+}(0)$. This is of course possible provided that $\overline{p}_{H,+}(0) \leq \overline{\overline{p}}_{H,+}(0)$. Finally, this last inequality is equivalent to

$$\frac{2(1-L^2)}{4(1-L) + L(1+L)} \leq \frac{2(4-L)(1-L^2)}{2[2(2-L)(1+L) - L^2(1-L)]}.$$

Algebraic manipulation indicates that this is equivalent to:

$0 > 3L^3 - 13L^2 + 20L - 8$. Numerical analysis reveals that this inequality if true for $L \leq L^* \approx .6042$. There is also the alternative condition that needs to be examined: $\overline{\overline{p}}_{H,-}(0) < p < \overline{p}_{H,-}(0)$, However this solution is impossible as $\overline{\overline{p}}_{H,-}(0) = \overline{p}_{H,-}(0) = 0$. Q.e.d.

Proof of Theorem 4: We prove Theorem 4 in a series of simple steps. The first lemma rules out the possibility that the high-quality firm "burns" an unnecessary amount of money in advertising campaigns to signal its type.

Lemma 5: Any separating profile $((\hat{p}_H, \hat{A}_H), (\hat{p}_L, \hat{A}_L))$ with $\hat{A}_H > \max\{\overline{A}_H(\hat{p}_H), 0\}$ is destabilized.

Proof: Almost trivial. Take any separating profile with $\hat{A}_H > \max\{\overline{A}_H(\hat{p}_H), 0\}$. Then there exists an alternative pair $(p^0, A^0) = (\hat{p}_H, \hat{A}_H - \epsilon)$, with $\epsilon > 0$, which is in the interior of $\mathcal{L}^S(L) \cap H^S(L)$. Hence by REDE $\mu((\hat{p}_H, \hat{A}_H - \epsilon), (\hat{p}_L, \hat{A}_L)) = 1$, and the posterior belief is that the high-quality firm has chosen $(\hat{p}_H, \hat{A}_H - \epsilon)$ with probability one, while the low-quality firm has chosen $(\hat{p}_L, \hat{A}_L)$ with probability one. Thus, the high-quality firm strictly prefers $(\hat{p}_H, \hat{A}_H - \epsilon)$

to $(\hat{p}_H, \hat{A}_H)$, since payoffs have increased by $\epsilon > 0$. Hence, the profile $((\hat{p}_H, \hat{A}_H), (\hat{p}_L, \hat{A}_L))$ is destabilized. Q.e.d.

The lemma is illustrated in Figure A1 where the x_i's, $i=1,2,3$, are examples of the choice of the high-quality firm in the separating profiles under scrutiny. Panel (a) relates to the case where pure price separation is possible ($L < L^*$), and Panel (b) to the case where pure price separation is impossible.

[Figure A1 about here]

The next lemma restricts the set of prices, $\hat{p}_H$, in the case where pure price separation is possible.

Lemma 6: Suppose that $L \leq L^*$. Then any separating profile

$((\hat{p}_H, \hat{A}_H), (\hat{p}_L, \hat{A}_L))$ with $(\hat{p}_H, \hat{A}_H) = (\hat{p}_H, 0)$ where $\hat{p}_H > \overline{p}_{H,+}(0)$ is

destabilized.

Proof: (Sketch) Take a profile $((\hat{p}_H, 0), (\hat{p}_L, 0))$ with $\hat{p}_H \in (\overline{p}_{H,+}, \overline{\overline{p}}_{H,+}]$ and $\hat{p}_L = (L/2)\hat{p}_H$. We leave to the reader the simple proof that $\overline{p}_{H,+}(0)$ is the unique best response of the high-quality firm to $\hat{p}_L$. The details can be found in Hertzendorf and Overgaard (1998). Q.e.d.

Referring to panel (b) of Figure A1 (e.g. x_4), the proof of Lemma 6 amounts to showing that $(\hat{p}_H, 0)$ with $\hat{p}_H > \overline{p}_{H,+}(0)$ gives strictly lower profits to the high-quality firm than any $(\hat{p}_H - \epsilon, 0)$, for $\epsilon > 0$ and $\hat{p}_H - \epsilon \geq \overline{p}_{H,+}(0)$. Since $(\hat{p}_H - \epsilon, 0) \in \mathcal{L}^S(L) \cap H^S(L)$, REDE implies that $\mu((\hat{p}_H - \epsilon, 0), (\hat{p}_L, 0)) = 1$ and it follows that the profits of the high-quality firm are strictly decreasing in $\hat{p}_H$ on the interval $[\overline{p}_{H,+}(0), \overline{\overline{p}}_{H,+}(0)]$ holding beliefs fixed (the high-quality firm is believed to be high quality).

Combining Lemma 5 and Lemma 6 leaves us with the candidates $(\hat{p}_H, \overline{A}_H(\hat{p}_H)) \in \mathcal{L}^S(L) \cap H^S(L)$ for separating strategies of the high-quality firm that satisfy REDE. These are points along the segment $\overline{A}_H(p)$ in the admissible set $\mathcal{L}^S(L) \cap H^S(L)$ (see Figure A1). If $\overline{A}_H(p)$ intersects the price axis while it is below $\overline{\overline{A}}_H(p)$ (i.e., when $L < L^*$) this set will include $(\overline{p}_{H,+}(0), 0)$. We are now ready to proceed to our main result on separating equilibria. With the imposition of

REDE, a separating profile $((\hat{p}_H, \hat{A}_H), (\hat{p}_L, \hat{A}_L))$, with $(\hat{P}_H, \hat{A}_H) \in \mathcal{L}^S(L) \cap H^S(L)$ and $(\hat{p}_L, \hat{A}_L) = ((L/2)\hat{p}_H, 0)$ must be supported by beliefs that satisfy $\mu((p, A), (\hat{p}_L, \hat{A}_L)) = 1$ for all $(p, A) \in \mathcal{L}^S(L) \cap H^S(L)$ and $\mu((p, A), (\hat{p}_L, \hat{A}_L)) = 0$ for all $(p, A) \notin \mathcal{L}^S(L) \cap H^S(L)$, where the latter part rules out deviations by the high-quality firm to price-advertising pairs which are part of no separating equilibrium. Hence, $(\hat{p}_H, \hat{A}_H)$ must form a best response to $\hat{p}_L = (L/2)\hat{p}_H$ and $\hat{A}_L = 0$. Generally, $(\hat{p}_H, \hat{A}_H)$ must be a maximizer of $\Pi_H(p, \hat{p}_L, A, 1, L)$ on $\mathcal{L}^S(L) \cap H^S(L)$. However, Lemma 5 and 6 enable use to write this as the simple maximization problem:

$$\max_p \Pi_H(p, \hat{p}_L, \overline{A}_H(p), 1, L) \quad s.t. \ 0 \le \overline{A}_H(p) \le \overline{\overline{A}}_H(p) \ .$$

Since we can easily rule out that any maximizer is less than or equal to $\hat{p}_L$, we have

$$\Pi_H((p, \hat{p}_L, \overline{A}_H(p), 1, L) = p\left(1 - \frac{p - \hat{p}_L}{1 - L}\right) - \overline{A}_H(p) \ .$$

Further, define $\tilde{\pi}_H(p; \hat{p}_L) \equiv p\left(1 - \frac{p - \hat{p}_L}{1 - L}\right)$. Hence,

$$\Pi_H(p, \hat{p}_L, \overline{A}_H(p), 1, L) = \tilde{\pi}_H(p; \hat{p}_L) - \overline{A}_H(p)$$

and we seek to maximize this subject to $0 \le \overline{A}_H(p) \le \overline{\overline{A}}_H(p)$. We note that

$$\frac{d\Pi_H}{dp} = \frac{d\tilde{\pi}_H(p; \hat{p}_L)}{dp} - \frac{d\overline{A}_H(p)}{dp} = \left[1 + \frac{\hat{p}_L}{1 - L} - \frac{2p}{1 - L}\right] - \left[(1/2) - \frac{4(1 - L) + L(1 + L)}{2(1 - L^2)} p\right]$$

Let us initially, abstract from the constraint. Then for $(\hat{p}_H, \overline{A}_H(\hat{p}_H))$ to be a best response to $\hat{p}_L = (L/2)\hat{p}_H$ we must have

$$\frac{d\Pi_H(\hat{p}_H, (L/2)\hat{p}_H, \overline{A}_H(\hat{p}_H), 1, L)}{dp} = 0 \quad \text{or} \quad \frac{d\tilde{\pi}_H(\hat{p}_H; (L/2)\hat{p}_H)}{dp} = \frac{d\overline{A}_H(\hat{p}_H)}{dp} \ .$$

This requires $\hat{p}_H = (1 - L^2)/(2L(3 - L)) \equiv \tilde{p}_H(L)$. Hence if the constraint $0 \le \overline{A}_H(\tilde{p}_H(L)) \le \overline{\overline{A}}_H(\tilde{p}_H(L))$ is non-binding or binding with equality, then the unique maximizer on $\mathcal{L}^S(L) \cap H^S(L)$ is $(\hat{p}_H, \hat{A}_H) = (\tilde{p}_H(L), \overline{A}_H(\tilde{p}_H(L)))$ with which is associated $(\hat{p}_L, \hat{A}_L) = ((L/2)\tilde{p}_H(L), 0)$. Let us consider the constraints $\overline{A}_H(p) \ge 0$ and $\overline{A}_H(p) \le \overline{\overline{A}}_H(p)$. We can state

40

Lemma 7: $\bar{A}_H(p) \leq \bar{\bar{A}}_H(p)$ is never binding at $p = \tilde{p}_H(L)$.

Proof: Using the definitions $\bar{\bar{A}}_H(p) \geq \bar{A}_H(p)$ reduces to $p \leq [(2-L)(1-L^2)] / [L(5-4L+L^2)] \equiv p^0(L)$. We leave it to the reader to check that $p^0(L) > \tilde{p}_H(L)$ for all $L \in (0,1)$. Hence, $\bar{A}_H(\tilde{p}_H(L)) < \bar{\bar{A}}_H(\tilde{p}_H(L))$. Q.e.d.

To consider $0 \leq \bar{A}_H(p)$, let us first define $L^{**} \equiv \{L \mid \tilde{p}_H(L) = \bar{p}_{H,+}(0)\}$.[24] Then we can state

Lemma 8: $0 \leq \bar{A}_H(p)$ is binding at $p = \tilde{p}_H(L)$ if and only if $L \geq L^{**}$.

The upshot of Lemma 7 and 8 is that only the non-negativity constraint on advertising may be binding at the optimum. Combining this with Lemma 6 we conclude that if the non-negativity constraint is binding, then the unique maximizer (the unique best response) on

the admissible set $\mathcal{L}^S(L) \cap H^S(L)$ is $(\hat{p}_H, \hat{A}_H) = (\bar{p}_{H,+}(0), 0)$ with which

is associated a unique $(\hat{p}_L, \hat{A}_L) = ((L/2)\bar{p}_{H,+}(0), 0)$.[25] This completes the proof of Theorem 4. Q.e.d.

Proof of Theorem 5: First we note that an examination of our profit functions reveal that payoffs at any pooling equilibrium are (by construction) identical. Hence, if out-of-equilibrium beliefs are impartial it must be the case that for any defection (p', A'), $\mu((p', A'), (\hat{p}, \hat{A})) = 1/2$. It should be obvious that advertising cannot be sustained in an equilibrium. Suppose instead that $S_Q = (\hat{p}, \hat{A})$, $\hat{A} > 0$ were part of a pooling equilibrium. This could not be an optimal strategy for either firm since $\Pi_Q(\hat{p}, \hat{p}, 0, 1/2, L) > \Pi_Q(\hat{p}, \hat{p}, \hat{A}, 1/2, L)$. That is, given impartial out-of-equilibrium beliefs, advertising is an unnecessary expense since it is not necessary to sustain consumer beliefs.

In a similar vein, consider an arbitrary pooling equilibrium where $\tilde{S}_Q = (\hat{p}, 0)$ with $\hat{p} > 0$. Given impartial out-of-equilibrium beliefs, this strategy could not be optimal since for any $\hat{p} > 0$ there exists an ϵ sufficiently small so that

---

[24] Recall that $L^{**} \equiv 0.29584 < L^* = 0.6042$.

[25] Recall from the definition that $\bar{p}_{H,+}(0)$ is a function of L.

$\Pi_Q(\hat{p}-\epsilon,\hat{p},0,1/2,L) > \Pi_Q(\hat{p},\hat{p},0,1/2,L)$.

More formally, $lim_{\epsilon \downarrow 0}\ \Pi_Q(\hat{p}-\epsilon,\hat{p},0,1/2,L) = 2\,\Pi_Q(\hat{p},\hat{p},0,1/2,L)$.

In words, by slightly undercutting its rival's price a firm can capture all the market to itself and virtually double its profit. (Recall that at any pooling equilibrium the consumers divide their purchases equally (and randomly) between the two firms.)

Only when the price is already zero is it impossible to profitably undercut the price of one's rival. Hence, the only pooling equilibrium that can be sustained by impartial out-of-equilibrium beliefs is $S_H = S_L = (0,0)$. Q.e.d.

References

Bagwell, K. (1992), Pricing to Signal Product Line Quality, *Journal of Economics and Management Strategy* 1: 154-174.

Bagwell, K. and G. Ramey (1991), Oligopoly Limit Pricing, *Rand Journal of Economics* 22: 155-172.

Bagwell, K and M.H. Riordan (1991), High and Declining Prices Signal Product Quality, *American Economic Review* 81: 224-239.

Cho, I.-K. and D.M. Kreps (1987), Signaling Games and Stable Equilibria, *Quarterly Journal of Economics* 102:179-221.

Cho, I.-K. and J. Sobel (1990), Strategic Stability and Uniqueness in Signaling Games, *Journal of Economic Theory* 50: 381-413.

Gabszewicz, J.-J. and I. Grilo (1992), Price Competition when Consumers Are Uncertain about which Firm Sells which Quality, *Journal of Economics and Management Strategy* 1: 628-650.

Gabszewicz, J.-J. and J.-F. Thisse (1979), Price Competition, Quality and Income Disparities, *Journal of Economic Theory* 20: 340-359.

Gabszewicz, J.-J. and J.-F. Thisse (1980), Entry (and Exit) in a Differentiated Industry, *Journal of Economic Theory* 22: 327-338.

Hertzendorf, M.N. (1990), A Model of Signaling Product Quality, University of Rochester, Department of Economics, Working Paper #216.

Hertzendorf, M.N. (1993), I'm not a High-Quality Firm - but I Play One on TV, *Rand Journal of Economics* 24: 236-247.

Hertzendorf, M.N. (1996), A Game Theory Model of Celebrity Endorsements, Federal Trade Commission, Bureau of Economics, Working Paper #211.

Hertzendorf, M.N. and P.B. Overgaard (1998), Will the High-Quality Producer Please Stand Up? - A Model of Duopoly Signaling, Centre for Industrial Economics, University of Copenhagen, Discussion Paper 98-04.

43

Horstman, I. and G. MacDonald (1994), When is Advertising a Signal of Product Quality?, *Journal of Economics and Management Strategy* 3: 561-584.

Kreps, D.M. and R. Wilson (1982), Sequential Equilibria, *Econometrica* 50: 863-894.

Lutz, N.A. (1989), Warranties and Signals under Consumer Moral Hazard, *Rand Journal of Economics* 20: 239-255.

Matthews, S.A. and D. Fertig (1990), Advertising Signals of Product Quality, Northwestern University, CMSEMS Discussion Paper No. 881.

Milgrom, P. and J. Roberts (1986), Price and Advertising Signals of Product Quality, *Journal of Political Economy* 94: 796-821.

Overgaard, P.B. (1993), Prices as a Signal of Quality: A discussion of Equilibrium concepts in Signaling Games, *European Journal of Political Economy* 9: 483-504.

Overgaard, P.B. (1994), Equilibrium Effects of Potential Entry when Prices Signal Quality, *European Economic Review* 38: 367-383.

Ramey, G. (1987), Product Quality Signaling and Market Performance, Stanford University, IMSSS Technical Report No. 504.

Schultz, C. (1996), Polarization and Inefficient Policies, *Review of Economic Studies* 63: 331-344.

Shaked, A. and J. Sutton (1982), Relaxing Price Competition through Product Differentiation, *Review of Economic Studies* 49: 3-13.

Shaked, A. and J. Sutton (1983), Natural Oligopolies, *Econometrica* 51: 1469-1484.

Figure 1

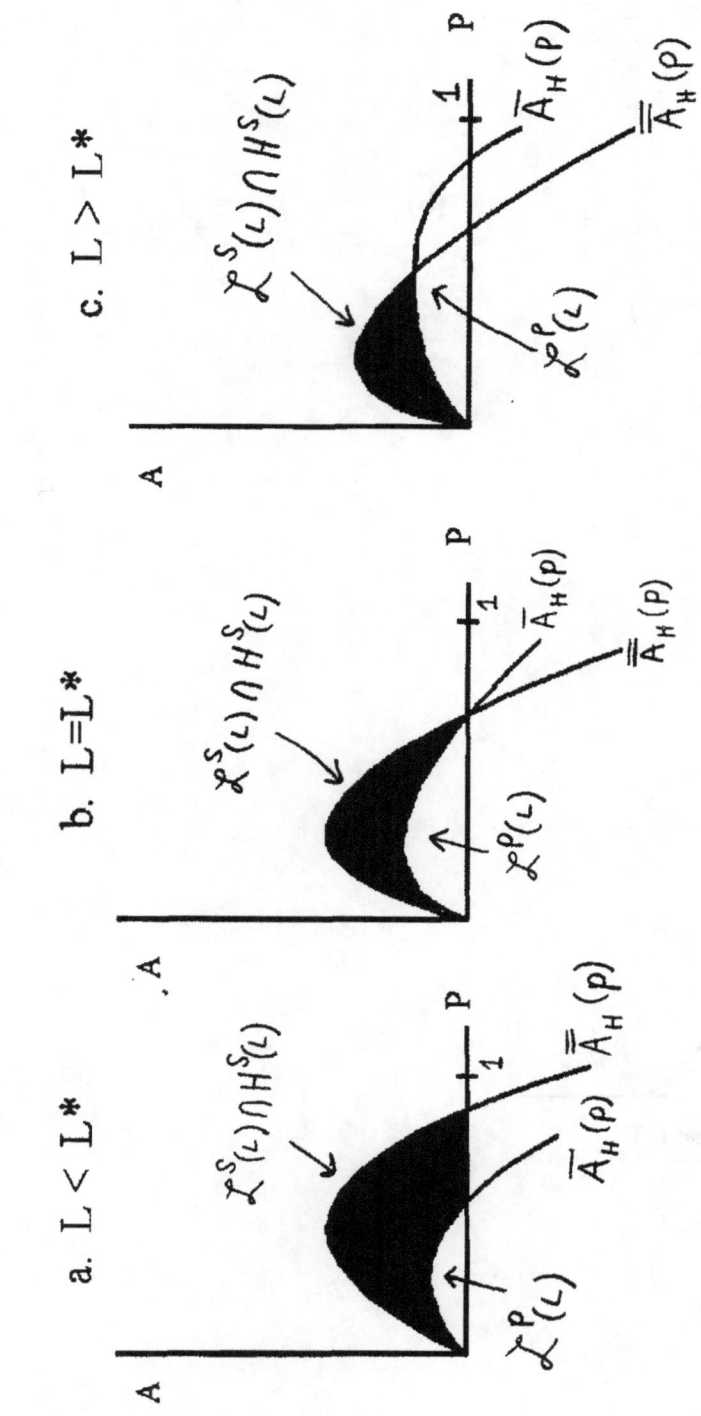

Figure 2

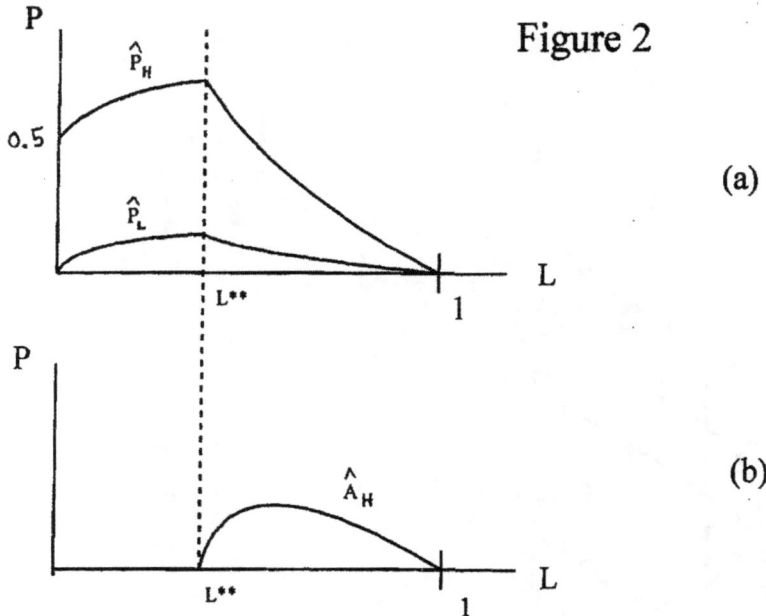

(a)

(b)

Figure 3

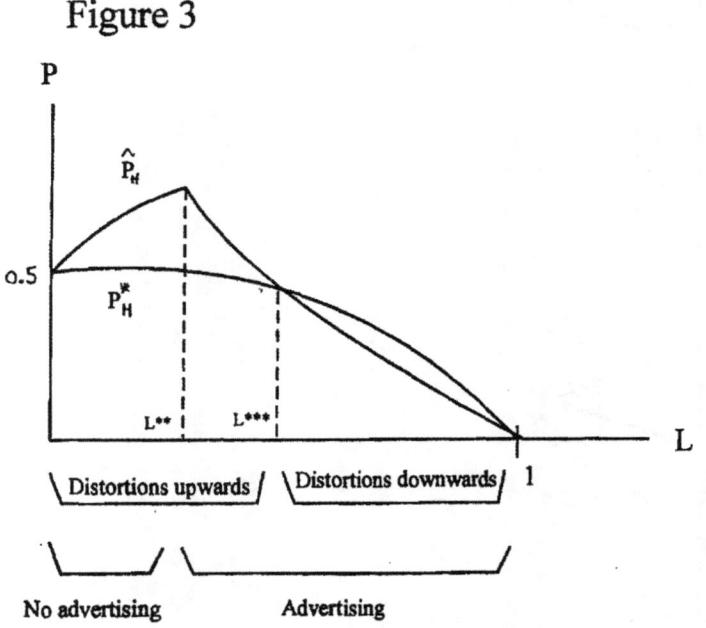

Figure A1   a. L < L *

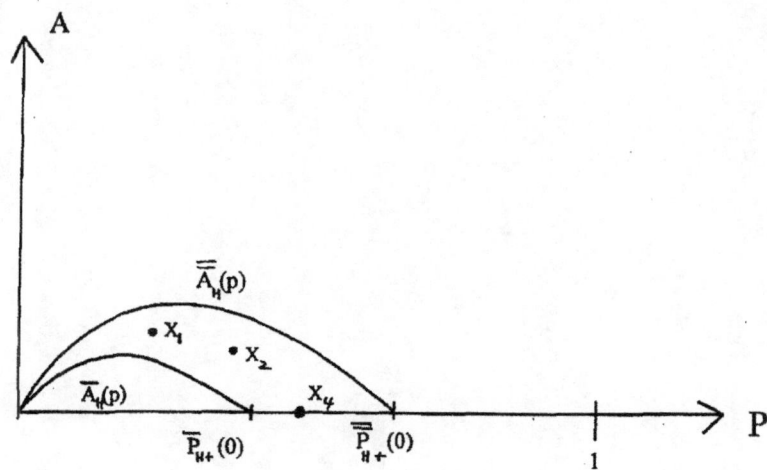

Figure A1   b. L > L *

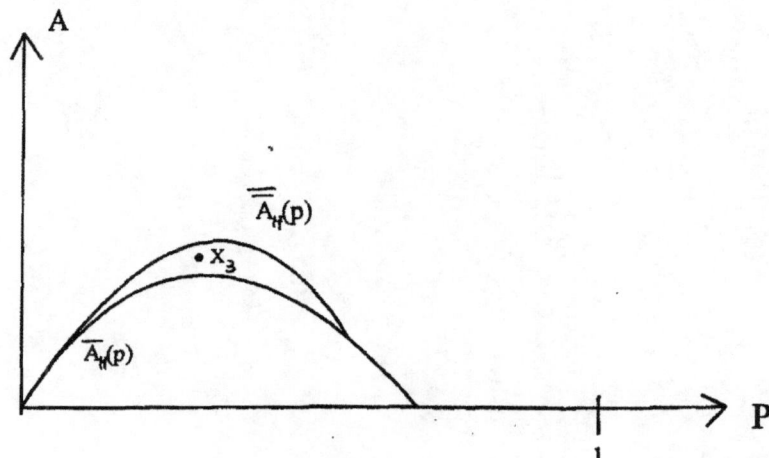